WITHDRAWN AND DONATED FOR SALE

Money

by Jennifer Waters

Content and Reading Adviser: Mary Beth Fletcher, Ed.D.
Educational Consultant/Reading Specialist
The Carroll School, Lincoln, Massachusetts

COMPASS POINT BOOKS

Minneapolis, Minnesota

Compass Point Books
3722 West 50th Street, #115
Minneapolis, MN 55410

Visit Compass Point Books on the Internet at *www.compasspointbooks.com*
or e-mail your request to *custserv@compasspointbooks.com*

Photographs ©: Lee White/Corbis, cover; EyeWire/Getty Images, 5, 8; TRIP, 7, 19; Imageselect, 9, 10, 12, 16; TRIP/H. Cundell, 11; Brian A. Vikander/Corbis, 13; TRIP/H. Rogers, 14, 15; Owen Franken/Corbis, 17; Digital Vision, 18; J.C. Carton/European Central Bank/Bruce Coleman Inc., 20; Bob Krist/Corbis, 21.

Project Manager: Rebecca Weber McEwen
Editor: Heidi Schoof
Photo Researcher: Image Select International Limited
Photo Selectors: Rebecca Weber McEwen and Heidi Schoof
Designer: Jaime Martens

Library of Congress Cataloging-in-Publication Data

Waters, Jennifer.
  Money / by Jennifer Waters.
     p. cm. — (Spyglass books)
Summary: A simple introduction to various types of currency used around the world.
Includes bibliographical references and index.
  ISBN 0-7565-0374-4 (hardcover)
  1. Money—Juvenile literature. [1. Money.] I. Title. II. Series.
  HG221.5 .W38 2002
  332.4—dc21
                                    2002002555

© 2003 by Compass Point Books
All rights reserved. No part of this book may be reproduced without written permission from the publisher. The publisher takes no responsibility for the use of any of the materials or methods described in this book, nor for the products thereof.
Printed in the United States of America.

Contents

Money 4
United States 6
Mexico 8
Brazil 10
Cameroon 12
England 14
Turkey 16
Japan 18
Europe 20
Glossary 22
Learn More 23
Index 24

Money

People all over the world use money to buy things. Different countries use different kinds of money.

United States

In the United States, people pay with dollars. One hundred cents equal one dollar.

United States

Mexico

In *Mexico,* people pay with pesos. One dollar equals about nine pesos. A peso is worth about 10 cents.

Pesos

Mexico

Pronunciation Guide
peso—*pay-so*

9

Brazil

In *Brazil,* people pay with reales.
One dollar equals about three reales.
A real is worth about 32 cents.

Reales

Brazil

Pronunciation Guide
reales—*ray-al-es*

Cameroon

In *Cameroon,* people pay with francs. One dollar equals about 750 francs. A franc is worth less than a cent.

Francs

Cameroon

Pronunciation Guide
franc—*frank*

13

England

In *England,* people pay with pounds. One dollar equals more than half of one pound. A pound is worth about $1.50.

A pound

Turkey

In *Turkey*, people pay with lira. One dollar equals more than a million lira. A lira is worth less than a cent.

Lira

Turkey

Pronunciation Guide
lira—*lee-rah*

17

Japan

In *Japan,* people
pay with yen.
One dollar equals
more than one hundred yen.
A yen is worth
less than a cent.

Yen

Europe

In most of **Europe,** people pay with euros.
One dollar equals about the same as a euro.
A euro is worth about the same as a dollar.

Euro

Europe

Pronunciation Guide
euro—*yu-roh*

Glossary

Brazil–a country on the continent called South America

Cameroon–a country on the continent called Africa

England–an island country off of the continent called Europe

Europe–one of the seven continents

Japan–an island country off of the continent called Asia

Mexico–a country on the continent called North America

Turkey–a country on the continents called Asia and Europe

Learn More

Books

Glass, Julie. *A Dollar for Penny.* New York: Random House, 2000.

Long, Lunette. *One Dollar: My First Book about Money.* Illustrated by Carol A. Camburn. Hauppauge, N. Y.: Barron's Educational Series, 1998.

Mitgutsch, Ali. *From Gold to Money.* Minneapolis, Minn.: Carolrhoda Books, 1984.

Web Sites

www.mmforkids.org/kids/kids_index.html

ustreas.gov/opc/opc0034.html

Index

dollar, 6, 8, 10, 12, 14, 16, 18, 20
euro, 20
franc, 12
lira, 16
peso, 8
pound, 14
real, 10
world, 4
yen, 18

GR: G
Word Count: 181

From Jennifer Waters

I live near the Rocky Mountains, but the ocean is my favorite place. I like to write songs and books. I hope you enjoyed this book.

BOSTON PUBLIC LIBRARY

3 9999 04720 550 3

DU 7/03